MW01243542

This Journal
Belongs To:

Made in the USA
Middletown, DE
11 August 2022

71172539R00070